W9-DJG-741

INSIDE THE
NFL

ATLANTA
FALCONS

BY ROBERT COOPER

SportsZone

An Imprint of Abdo Publishing
abdobooks.com

abdobooks.com

Published by Abdo Publishing, a division of ABDO, PO Box 398166, Minneapolis, Minnesota 55439. Copyright © 2020 by Abdo Consulting Group, Inc. International copyrights reserved in all countries. No part of this book may be reproduced in any form without written permission from the publisher. SportsZone™ is a trademark and logo of Abdo Publishing.

Printed in the United States of America, North Mankato, Minnesota
042019
092019

THIS BOOK CONTAINS
RECYCLED MATERIALS

Cover Photo: Rick Osentoski/AP Images
Interior Photos: Ryan Kang/AP Images, 5; David J. Phillip/AP Images, 7; Damian Strohmeyer/AP Images, 9; Patrick Smith/Getty Images Sport/Getty Images, 11; AP Images, 13; NFL Photos/AP Images, 15, 17, 19, 21, 43; Focus on Sport/Getty Images Sport/ Getty Images, 23, 25; Al Messerschmidt/AP Images, 27; David Durochik/AP Images, 29; Alan Mothner/AP Images, 31; John Bazemore/AP Images, 33; Darren Hauck/AP Images, 35; John Amis/AP Images, 39; Curtis Compton/Atlanta Journal-Constitution/AP Images, 40

Editor: Patrick Donnelly
Series Designer: Craig Hinton

Library of Congress Control Number: 2018965783

Publisher's Cataloging-in-Publication Data

Names: Cooper, Robert, author.
Title: Atlanta Falcons / by Robert Cooper
Description: Minneapolis, Minnesota: Abdo Publishing, 2020 | Series: Inside the NFL | Includes
 online resources and index.
Identifiers: ISBN 9781532118371 (lib. bdg.) | ISBN 9781532172557 (ebook) | ISBN
 9781644941010 (pbk.)
Subjects: LCSH: Atlanta Falcons (Football team)--Juvenile literature. | National Football League--
 Juvenile literature. | Football teams--Juvenile literature. | American football--Juvenile
 literature.
Classification: DDC 796.33264--dc23

TABLE OF
CONTENTS

CHAPTER 1
SO CLOSE 4

CHAPTER 2
GETTING STARTED 12

CHAPTER 3
PLAYOFFS, HERE WE COME 18

CHAPTER 4
BECOMING SUPER 26

CHAPTER 5
FALCONS SOAR 34

TIMELINE   42
QUICK STATS   44
QUOTES AND ANECDOTES   45
GLOSSARY   46
MORE INFORMATION   47
ONLINE RESOURCES   47
INDEX   48
ABOUT THE AUTHOR   48

SO CLOSE

With a trip to the Super Bowl on the line, things were looking good for the Atlanta Falcons. It was the National Football Conference (NFC) Championship Game on January 22, 2017. The Falcons were playing in front of their home fans in the comfort of the Georgia Dome. And halfway through the second quarter, they led the Green Bay Packers 17–0.

But some Falcons felt uneasy. Players who were on the 2012 team were in the exact situation four seasons earlier. Those players included Matt Ryan, who had been the Falcons quarterback since 2008.

In January 2013, the Falcons led the San Francisco 49ers 17–0 in the second quarter of the NFC Championship Game. That was also in the Georgia Dome. Those Falcons were shut out in the second half and lost the game 28–24.

Matt Ryan looks for a receiver in the NFC Championship Game against Green Bay in January 2017.

That loss set the franchise back. Atlanta missed the playoffs each of the next three seasons. The Falcons did not even have a winning record in that span. A 6–10 mark in 2014 spelled the end for head coach Mike Smith. He was replaced by Dan Quinn, and the team rebounded to 8–8 in 2015.

The 2016 team was not expected to be much better. The Falcons were expected to have one of the worst records in the National Football League (NFL). Some experts picked the Falcons to finish 5–11. Instead they went 11–5 and made it back to the conference title game. Ryan had the best year of his career. He was named the league's Most Valuable Player (MVP).

The Falcons were determined to avoid repeating the mistakes they'd made in 2013, when they let the 49ers back into the game by allowing two touchdowns in the second quarter. This time around, the Falcons kept charging forward. In the last two minutes of the first half, Ryan led them on a 68-yard drive. It ended in a 5-yard touchdown pass to wide receiver Julio Jones with three seconds left. That made the score 24–0 at halftime.

Though Green Bay rallied a bit in the second half, Atlanta's lead never slipped below 22 points. Ryan played like an MVP. He threw four touchdown passes and ran for another score.

✗ Julio Jones (11) had a huge day as the Falcons battled for a spot in the Super Bowl.

Jones caught nine passes for 180 yards and two touchdowns. With a dominating 44–21 win, the Falcons were going to their second Super Bowl in team history.

The 2016 Falcons had the league's top-scoring offense. They had the league MVP at quarterback and two top receivers in Jones and Mohamed Sanu. They would be a tough matchup for any team.

But to win the Super Bowl, the Falcons had to defeat Tom Brady and the New England Patriots. The Patriots had the best defense in the league. And their offense was almost as good as Atlanta's. The Falcons led the NFL in points per game, but New England was third.

Uncharacteristically, both offenses struggled early. In the first quarter, only four plays were run in the opponent's half of the field. Then Atlanta's defense made a big play. Linebacker Deion Jones forced a fumble as New England was driving. The Falcons then mounted their own drive, going 71 yards for the first touchdown of the game, a 5-yard gain by running back Devonta Freeman.

The defense held the Patriots to three plays on their next drive. Atlanta then marched for another touchdown, a 19-yard pass from Ryan to rookie tight end Austin Hooper. The Patriots tried to answer, but Falcons cornerback Robert Alford intercepted Brady

RECORD-SETTING RYAN

Matt Ryan threw for 392 yards in the NFC Championship Game against the Packers. That was the second-highest total for a playoff game in Falcons history. He fell four yards short of matching his own record total of 396, which he posted in the previous NFC Championship against the 49ers. Ryan holds Atlanta's career records for passing yards in both the playoffs and in the regular season.

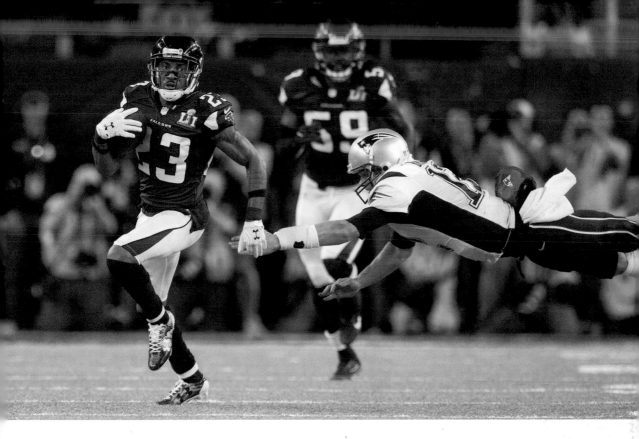

✕ Robert Alford (23) races down the sideline with an interception as Tom Brady comes up short on a diving tackle attempt.

and returned it 82 yards for a touchdown. With just over two minutes to play in the first half, Atlanta led 21–0.

New England got on the board with a field goal with five seconds left. But there was no question who was dominating Super Bowl LI. Atlanta was in line for its first NFL championship.

The Falcons came out firing in the second half as well. On their second drive of the half, Ryan found Tevin Coleman for a 6-yard touchdown to make it 28–3. With just over 23 minutes remaining, it would take a miracle for New England to come back.

Unfortunately for the Falcons, miracles were Brady's specialty. On their next three drives, the Patriots scored two touchdowns and kicked a field goal to make the score 28–20. The Falcons had no answer. They were not turning the ball over. But they also could not move the ball or run the clock down. Whenever they gave the ball back to the Patriots, Brady led them right down the field.

He did so again with 3:30 to go. The drive started on the New England 9-yard line. But Brady steadily moved the Patriots 90 yards to the Atlanta goal line. With one minute left, running back James White ran it in for a score. Brady then found wide receiver Danny Amendola for the two-point conversion to tie the game.

The Falcons were stunned. No team had ever come back from more than 10 points down in a Super Bowl. They still could win in overtime. But they never got the chance.

The Patriots won the overtime coin toss. Brady marched them 75 yards in less than four minutes. White burrowed two yards for another touchdown, and the game was over. The Falcons had blown the biggest lead in Super Bowl history.

✗ Devonta Freeman (24), punter Matt Bosher (5), and the rest of the Falcons sideline react in disbelief after losing the Super Bowl in overtime.

At one point in the third quarter, statisticians gave Atlanta a 99.7 percent chance of winning.

After one of the most memorable seasons in team history, it was a devastating loss for the Falcons. The players and coaches would never forget it. But like they did after blowing the NFC Championship Game lead against the 49ers four years earlier, they had to put the loss behind them.

"I think you'll always have a little bit of that scar that kind of drives you," Ryan said before the start of the next season. "That's fine. Never let go of that, but our focus is 100 percent about what we're doing and what we're moving forward to."

CHAPTER 2

GETTING
STARTED

The Falcons' road to their first Super Bowl was not paved overnight. The team was born on June 30, 1965. Atlanta insurance executive Rankin M. Smith was the founder and owner of the Falcons. He became a hero to many when the NFL granted an expansion team to Georgia's biggest city.

Smith had been away from his office on the day of the announcement. When he returned to work the next day, more good news awaited him. More than 1,000 people had called the office to buy tickets. Football fans in Georgia were eager to fill Atlanta-Fulton County Stadium.

A contest to name the team was held over the next several weeks. A few fans had submitted the nickname "Falcons." Schoolteacher Julia Elliott of Griffin, Georgia,

NFL commissioner Pete Rozelle, left, presents a certificate of membership to Falcons owner Rankin M. Smith.

The National Football League
Certificate of Membership

This is to Certify That

The Atlanta Falcons Football Club

Owning and operating a Professional Football Club has by proper action
of The National Football League, been duly nominated and admitted into membership in that League and has complied with Article III.

This Certificate

Endorses the right of The Five Smiths, Inc. to represent the City of Atlanta,
Georgia in The National Football League in keeping with the provisions of its
Constitution and By-Laws.

This membership may be transferred or assigned in keeping with the provisions of
the Constitution and By-Laws of The National Football League.

explained her choice: "The Falcon is proud and dignified, with great courage and fight. It never drops prey. It is deadly and has a great sporting tradition." That was good enough to win over team officials.

Smith's next step was to name the team's first head coach. He chose Norb Hecker, a former assistant coach with the Green Bay Packers. The Falcons' preseason debut took place on August 27, 1966, in Columbia, South Carolina. On that day, Atlanta beat the San Francisco 49ers 24–17.

By the time the regular season began, the Falcons were faced with more difficult challenges. After losing their first nine games, they earned their first victory on November 20 in a 27–16 win over the New York Giants at Yankee Stadium.

TICKETS ANYONE?

The Falcons sold 45,000 season tickets their first season. Before that, the record for most season tickets sold for a first-year team was held by the Minnesota Vikings with 26,000 in 1961.

Linebacker Tommy Nobis, a former University of Texas standout, was the Falcons' first draft pick. His selection as the NFL Rookie of the Year provided the team with hope.

Unfortunately for their fans, the Falcons were not on the winning end of many games during their

✗ Linebacker Tommy Nobis, shown in 1968, was selected to the Pro Bowl five times with Atlanta.

first few years in the league. Their inaugural season in 1966 ended with a 3–11 record.

It got even worse in 1967, when Hecker's team finished 1–12–1. Just three games into the 1968 season, former NFL star quarterback Norm Van Brocklin replaced Hecker as coach. The results were not much better in Van Brocklin's first season, as the Falcons went 2–12.

In 1971 Van Brocklin had plenty of reasons to believe things were looking up for the Falcons. In February he had been elected to the Pro Football Hall of Fame for his play at quarterback with the Los Angeles Rams and Philadelphia Eagles. By December he was guiding the Falcons to their first winning season in team history. Atlanta finished with a 7–6–1 record.

NOT SO FAST

The NFL was not the only league that had its sights set on Atlanta. The American Football League (AFL) also believed that football would be a success in the city. In fact, two different groups reportedly applied for ownership of an AFL team in Atlanta. One group of Atlanta businessmen was awarded an AFL team on June 7, 1965.

NFL commissioner Pete Rozelle got word of the AFL's interest in Atlanta and quickly flew to the city. The NFL was very interested in placing a team in the South. Rozelle wanted to stop the rival league's claim on Atlanta.

Rozelle forced the city—which owned the stadium that the team would play in—to choose between the two leagues. A little more than three weeks later, insurance executive Rankin M. Smith spread word that the team would become a member of the NFL. Smith paid $8.5 million for the team.

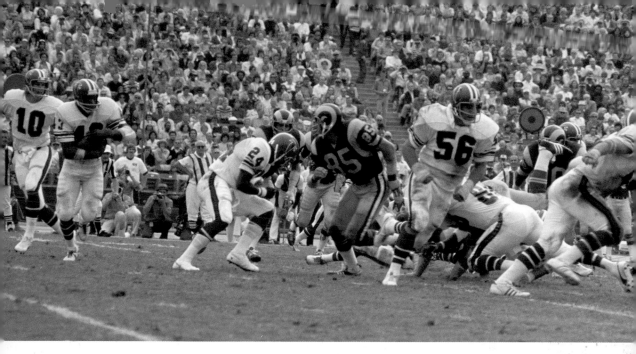

✕ The Falcons' Dave Hampton carries the ball against the Rams in 1975. Hampton ran for more than 1,000 yards that season.

The Van Brocklin era featured two winning seasons. The Falcons went 9–5 in 1973. However, eight games into the 1974 season, Van Brocklin was fired and replaced by defensive coordinator Marion Campbell. Back-to-back 4–10 seasons in 1975 and 1976 were highlighted mainly by running back Dave Hampton. He became the first Falcon to rush for 1,000 yards in a season when he chalked up 61 in the 1975 season finale. He ended the season with 1,002 yards.

A decade of struggles was about to end, however. Leeman Bennett, a former offensive assistant with the Los Angeles Rams, was hired as the Falcons' head coach in 1977. He would prove to be the man to guide Atlanta to the playoffs.

CHAPTER 3

PLAYOFFS, HERE WE COME

It did not take long to notice coach Leeman Bennett's impact on the Falcons when he arrived in 1977. A defense that had struggled in previous years suddenly was being compared to some of the NFL's best defenses of all time. Quarterback Steve Bartkowski, the first overall pick in the 1975 NFL Draft, began to thrive under Bennett's guidance. The Falcons were headed in the right direction.

Claude Humphrey, Atlanta's first-round draft pick in 1968, continued to excel at defensive end. Rolland Lawrence was a turnover threat at cornerback. In 1977 he intercepted seven passes and was named to the Pro Bowl. Lawrence's impact on the Falcons' defense did not go unnoticed during his time manning the corner, from 1973 to 1980. He started

Steve Bartkowski led the Falcons to their first playoff spot in 1978.

every game for seven seasons in a row and ended his career in Atlanta with 39 interceptions.

Defensive backs coach Jerry Glanville helped Bennett mold a group that put up some of the stingiest numbers ever seen in the NFL. In the three previous seasons, the Falcons had allowed opponents to score a combined 872 points—nearly 21 points per game. Those numbers changed quite a bit in 1977. In fact, the Falcons set the NFL's 14-game season record by allowing only 129 points that year—just over 9 points per game. The result was seven wins, the most for the team since 1973.

Bennett had made his mark. Over the next five years, the Falcons advanced to the playoffs three times. They went 9–7 in 1978, boosted by their first shutout ever—a 14–0 win over the Detroit Lions at Atlanta-Fulton County Stadium. A mid-December loss by Washington ensured the Falcons their first trip to the playoffs as a wild card.

GROWING PAINS

Steve Bartkowski's numbers were not so impressive at the beginning of his career in Atlanta. In his first four seasons combined, he threw 30 touchdown passes and 55 interceptions. But when he led the Falcons to their first division title in 1980, Bartkowski threw a team-record 31 touchdown passes and 16 interceptions.

✖ Leeman Bennett took over as the Falcons' head coach in 1977. His Atlanta teams made the playoffs three times in six seasons.

Bartkowski made a name for himself in his first playoff appearance, a home game against the Philadelphia Eagles. On a rain-soaked day, Bartkowski threw two touchdown passes in the game's final eight minutes to give Atlanta a 14–13 lead.

The Eagles missed a 34-yard field goal try in the closing seconds and the Falcons' first playoff victory was in the books. The win sent the Falcons on to the divisional round.

Against Dallas the next week, Atlanta led 20–13 at halftime. The Falcons' defense knocked star quarterback Roger Staubach out of the game before halftime. However, backup Danny White led Dallas to 14 unanswered points in the second half to post a 27–20 victory. The Falcons had the ball at the Cowboys' 32-yard line and faced a key fourth-and-one play in the fourth quarter. Dallas' defense held strong, and the Falcons were stuffed.

A 6–10 season in 1979 hardly set the stage for what was to come in 1980. Second-year running back William Andrews broke his own team record with 1,308 rushing yards. Wide receiver Alfred Jenkins tallied 1,035 receiving yards, another record. And Bartkowski

BIG BEN

Steve Bartkowski's fame grew extensively on November 12, 1978. Atlanta trailed New Orleans 17–13 with the ball at its own 43-yard line and time running out. On a play named "Big Ben Right," the Falcons' receivers all lined up on one side of the field. Bartkowski threw the ball to the New Orleans 15, where Falcons receiver Wallace Francis tipped the pass in the air. Teammate Alfred Jackson slipped behind a pile of players and caught the ball, then ran the rest of the way into the end zone, giving Atlanta a last-second victory.

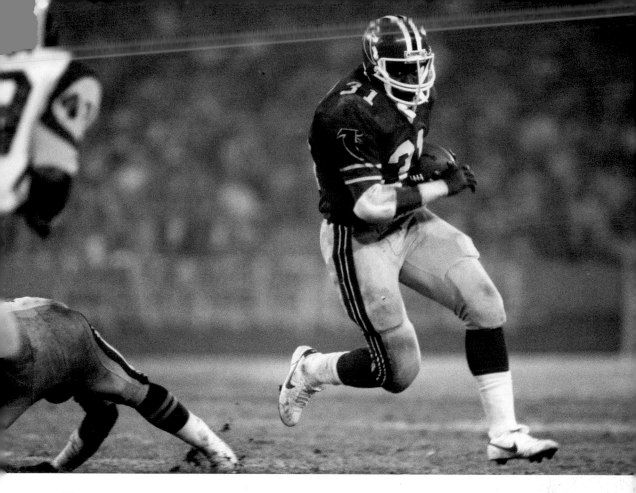

✗ William Andrews was a wrecking ball in the Falcons backfield.

set single-season team records with 3,544 passing yards and 31 touchdown passes.

The Falcons secured their first NFC West Division title with a 35–10 thumping of San Francisco on December 14. Bartkowski threw three touchdown passes, and Andrews rushed for more than 100 yards for the sixth time that season. The Falcons' twelfth victory of the season was also their ninth in a row. Both were club records.

BACKFIELD MATES

The duo of William Andrews and Gerald Riggs in Atlanta's backfield gave Falcons fans plenty to talk about. The two players first started doing damage together during the 1982 season, which was shortened due to a players' strike. In the first game after the strike, Andrews gained 207 total yards. Riggs, a rookie, scored his first two touchdowns in a 34–17 win over the Los Angeles Rams.

The Falcons went 4–12 in 1985, but the season was not without excitement. Riggs ran for 158 yards in the season finale. His 1,719 rushing yards that season led the NFC and were the most in team history until 1998.

In the divisional round of the playoffs against Dallas, Atlanta led 24–10 after three quarters. Still, the Falcons saw the Cowboys come back to win 30–27 in front of 60,022 people—Atlanta-Fulton County Stadium's largest crowd ever.

After a 7–9 season in 1981, Atlanta returned to the playoffs in 1982. That year, a strike by the NFL's players reduced the length of the regular season from 16 games to nine. Atlanta went 5–4 and advanced to the playoffs for the third time. At the Metrodome against Minnesota, Atlanta had a 21–16 lead after three quarters in the first-round game. The Vikings, however, came back to win 30–24.

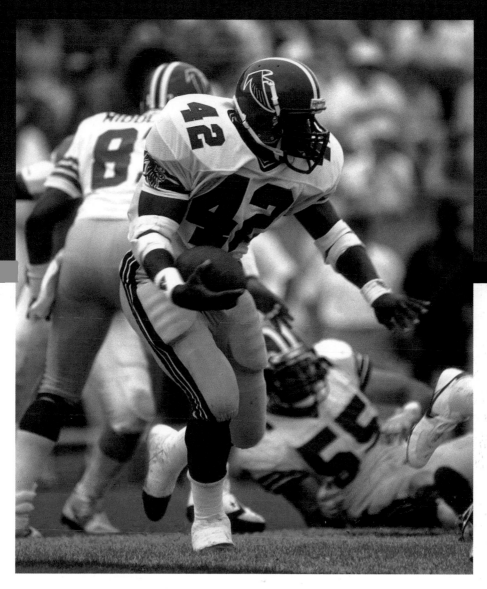

✗ In 1985 Gerald Riggs ran for 1,719 yards, a team record at the time.

Playoff opportunities, as the Falcons would learn in the coming seasons, are not chances to be taken lightly. Atlanta wouldn't be back in the postseason for nine years.

CHAPTER 4

BECOMING
SUPER

The Falcons went through some lean years after the strike-shortened season of 1982. They posted eight losing seasons in a row until head coach Jerry Glanville helped turn things around in 1991.

The Falcons put together a five-game winning streak that year. They won eight of their final 11 games to earn a playoff spot with a 10–6 record. They won road games against all three of their division opponents.

The 1991 season was the Falcons' last at Atlanta-Fulton County Stadium. A sellout crowd watched as Atlanta topped the Seattle Seahawks 26–13 in the stadium finale to push the team's home winning streak to five games.

Deion Sanders joined the Falcons in 1989 and quickly became a standout punt and kick returner and cornerback.

A 27–20 victory at New Orleans in a wild-card playoff game set up a showdown at Washington in the divisional round. Former Falcon Gerald Riggs scored two touchdowns to help the host team to a 24–7 victory. Atlanta managed only 43 rushing yards, while Falcons quarterback Chris Miller threw four interceptions.

On September 6, 1992, the Falcons played their first game at the Georgia Dome. They scored on their first four possessions and beat the New York Jets 20–17.

The move into the Georgia Dome brought with it plenty of offensive firepower for the Falcons. They led the NFL in 1992 with a team-record 33 touchdown passes. Their 336 pass completions and 194 first downs also set team records. Wide receiver Andre Rison had a record 93 receptions in 1992. He also became the first player in NFL history with 300 catches in his first four years in the league.

However, all that offense added up to just six wins, a record they matched in 1993. The points continued to pile up, though.

PRIME TIME

In 1991 Falcons cornerback Deion "Prime Time" Sanders signed a baseball contract with the Atlanta Braves. He became the first pro athlete in 30 years to play two sports in the same city.

✕ Andre Rison represented the Falcons in four straight Pro Bowls beginning in 1990.

For the fourth season in a row, Atlanta scored more than 300 points. Rison set a team record among receivers with 15 touchdown catches. But a strong offense with a poor defense once again led to bad results for the Falcons. Glanville was fired after the season and replaced by former Falcons quarterback June Jones.

Jones had an unremarkable three-year tenure, going 7–9, 9–7, and 3–13. In 1995, however, the Falcons did pull off an impressive Georgia Dome moment to reach the playoffs. Needing a win to qualify for the postseason, the Falcons edged defending Super Bowl champion San Francisco 28–27 on Christmas Eve. Quarterback Bobby Hebert threw two touchdown passes to Terance Mathis. Mathis found his way into the end zone with 1:45 to play for the game winner.

The Falcons earned a playoff trip. However, they were handed a 37–20 loss at Green Bay. After a 3–13 season in 1996, Jones was replaced as head coach by Dan Reeves, a Georgia native who would lead the Falcons to new heights.

Reeves had coached the Denver Broncos to three Super Bowls. His first Falcons team started 1–7 but won six of its final eight games behind a Pro Bowl effort from quarterback Chris Chandler and a team-record 55 sacks on defense. It was a sign of good things to come.

The "Dirty Birds," as they became known, launched into flight in the 1998 season. On November 8, the Falcons forced five turnovers and limited the New England Patriots to a record-low 18 rushing yards. All the buzz, however, was about their new end zone dance. Tight end O. J. Santiago and running

Falcons tight end O. J. Santiago does the "Dirty Bird" dance after a touchdown in 1998. Atlanta went 14–2 that season.

back Jamal Anderson were the ringleaders of the move. They got plenty of practice that day with two touchdowns apiece.

The Falcons put an exclamation point on their season with a 38–16 victory over the Miami Dolphins. That gave them a club-record 14–2 record, including a perfect 8–0 mark at home for the first time. The Falcons edged San Francisco 20–18 in

ANDERSON'S A GAMER

Jamal Anderson rushed for 5,336 yards and 34 touchdowns in an eight-year career with Atlanta. He ran for 1,846 yards in the Super Bowl season in 1998. Through 2018 only 15 players had rushed for more yards in an NFL season. Anderson, who played at the University of Utah, was not selected until the seventh round of the 1994 NFL Draft. He rushed for 1,000 yards in four different seasons for the Falcons before suffering a career-ending knee injury in 2001.

their playoff opener. That set them up for a date with the 15–1 Minnesota Vikings in the NFC Championship Game.

Few observers gave the Falcons much chance to win. The Vikings had scored an NFL-record 556 points in 1998. And they jumped out to a 20–7 lead in the first half. But the Falcons offense chipped away at the lead.

Vikings kicker Gary Anderson had not missed a field goal that season. But with a chance to extend the Vikings' 27–20 lead late in the fourth quarter, Anderson's field-goal attempt sailed wide left. The Falcons then took the ball and marched 71 yards to tie the game. It went into overtime.

Minnesota won the coin toss, but both teams were forced to punt on their first possessions. The Vikings could not move the ball again and had to punt it back. Chandler then drove the

✘ Atlanta's Jamal Anderson scored 16 touchdowns in 1998.

Falcons deep into Vikings territory. Kicker Morten Andersen lined up for a 38-yard field goal. He drilled it down the middle. The Falcons were headed to their first Super Bowl in Miami.

That's where the party ended for the Falcons. John Elway and the Denver Broncos won their second title in a row with a 34–19 defeat of the Falcons. Elway picked up the Super Bowl MVP Award in his final NFL game.

FALCONS SOAR

Even though Atlanta lost, just making the Super Bowl was the greatest achievement in Falcons history. The memories of that team live on with Falcons fans. But the team could not maintain that level of success. It followed its Super Bowl season with records of 5–11 and 4–12.

However, help was on the way. Atlanta made a deal with the San Diego Chargers to secure the rights to the number one pick in the 2001 NFL Draft. The Falcons selected Michael Vick. He was a quarterback out of Virginia Tech who could pass and run well. He would play six seasons with Atlanta.

In February 2002, Arthur Blank bought the Falcons from longtime owner Rankin M. Smith. Blank was a cofounder of the Home Depot store chain.

Quarterback Michael Vick breaks away from Green Bay defenders in the Falcons' playoff win in January 2003.

In his second season, Vick led the Falcons to a 9–6–1 record and a wild-card playoff berth. Atlanta defeated Green Bay 27–7 to become the first team ever to beat the Packers at home in a playoff game. The Falcons lost at Philadelphia 20–6 in the next round.

Reeves stepped down as head coach toward the end of the 2003 season. Former San Francisco defensive coordinator Jim Mora Jr. became Atlanta's coach in 2004. The Falcons went 11–5 and won the NFC South Division title in Mora's first season. In the playoffs, Atlanta routed visiting St. Louis 47–17 in the divisional round before losing to host Philadelphia 27–10 in the NFC Championship Game.

In April 2007, Vick was accused of being involved in an illegal dogfighting operation. It had been running in several states for more than five years. In August 2007, Vick pleaded guilty to federal felony charges. He admitted in court documents that he was involved in the dogfighting operation.

MICHAEL VICK

Michael Vick's best season came in 2004. His 902 rushing yards was the third-highest total by a quarterback in NFL history. In the playoffs, he guided the Falcons to their second NFC Championship Game. Vick ran for 119 yards in a divisional playoff win over St. Louis. Against Philadelphia in the NFC Championship Game, Vick managed only 26 rushing yards in Atlanta's loss.

He served 21 months in prison, followed by two months in home confinement, and the Falcons released him.

Before he served his prison sentence, the three-time Pro Bowl selection had passed for 11,505 yards and ran for another 3,859 in the equivalent of about five full seasons for the Falcons. The sudden loss of Vick was a shock.

Fortunately, the Falcons found his successor right away. Quarterback Matt Ryan was the third overall pick in the 2008 NFL Draft. He and new coach Mike Smith led the Falcons to the playoffs in 2008. Ryan was named the NFL Offensive Rookie of the Year and Smith the NFL Coach of the Year in 2008. The duo became the foundation of Atlanta's next championship-level teams.

Running back Michael Turner was another major contributor. The Falcons signed Turner in 2008 from the Chargers. His 1,699 yards in 2008 were the third-most in team history. In five years with Atlanta, he became one of the top running backs in franchise history. Turner posted three seasons of 1,300 yards or more.

The Falcons had a breakout year in 2010, going 13–3 and winning the NFC South Division for the first time in six years. Receiver Roddy White caught a league-leading 115 passes for

1,389 yards. The team was strong on defense too, allowing the fifth-fewest points in the NFL.

But Atlanta was overwhelmed by Green Bay in the playoffs. After the Falcons took a 14–7 lead, the Packers scored 28 points in the second quarter and cruised to a 48–21 victory.

The Falcons suffered an even worse playoff defeat the next year. They did not score a single point on offense in a 24–2 loss to the New York Giants.

The 2012 Falcons were again great in the regular season. They won 13 games and had a top-10 offense and defense. But they had done that before. What could they do in the playoffs? Behind two touchdown passes from Ryan, they built a 20–0 halftime lead over the Seattle Seahawks.

Then Seattle stormed back with 21 fourth-quarter points to take the lead with 34 seconds left. But Ryan wasn't going to let this one slip away. Two quick completions from

A NEW DOME

The Falcons closed out the Georgia Dome after the 2016 season. But they did not move far. Their new home was constructed right next door. Mercedes-Benz Stadium opened in 2017. Unlike the Georgia Dome, the roof on the new stadium can open. But it can remain closed in case of rain or extreme Atlanta heat. The stadium holds 71,000 fans.

✗ Matt Ryan, taken third overall by Atlanta in the 2008 draft, led the Falcons to the playoffs as a rookie.

Ryan—to Harry Douglas for 22 yards and to Tony Gonzalez for 19 more—put the Falcons at the Seattle 31 with 13 seconds left on the clock.

That was enough time for Matt Bryant. The Falcons kicker lined up for a 49-yard field-goal attempt. He nailed it, and the Falcons had their first playoff win since January 2005.

✗ Julio Jones (11) makes a diving catch for a touchdown against the Arizona Cardinals in 2018.

With a trip to the Super Bowl on the line, the Falcons blew another lead in the NFC Championship Game against the 49ers. But there was no comeback this time as they lost 28–24.

The Falcons brought in former Rams workhorse Steven Jackson to replace Turner at running back. They added defensive end Osi Umenyiora from the New York Giants to help the pass rush. But everything went wrong in 2013. The Falcons finished 4–12 and were the first team eliminated from playoff contention. They went 6–10 the next year, and Smith was replaced by Seattle defensive coordinator Dan Quinn.

One bright spot was the emergence of receiver Julio Jones. He was the Falcons' first-round draft pick in 2011. By 2014 he was the team's leading receiver with 1,593 yards. In 2015 he led the entire NFL with 1,871. That was a Falcons team record.

Quinn led the Falcons back to the Super Bowl after the 2016 season, thanks in large part to a high-scoring offense led by Ryan and Jones. As the offense declined in 2017, the defense improved to keep the Falcons in the playoffs. But they suffered another disappointing loss at Philadelphia in the divisional round.

In 2018 the defense took a big step back. Atlanta allowed 121 points in an early three-game losing streak. Later, a loss at Cleveland triggered a five-game losing skid that crushed Atlanta's playoff hopes.

Ryan threw for 4,924 yards and 35 touchdowns, narrowly missing his own records in both categories. And Jones once again was outstanding, leading the NFL with 1,677 receiving yards. After finishing the season 7–9, the Falcons replaced much of their coaching staff, but they gave Quinn another chance to turn it around in Atlanta.

TIMELINE

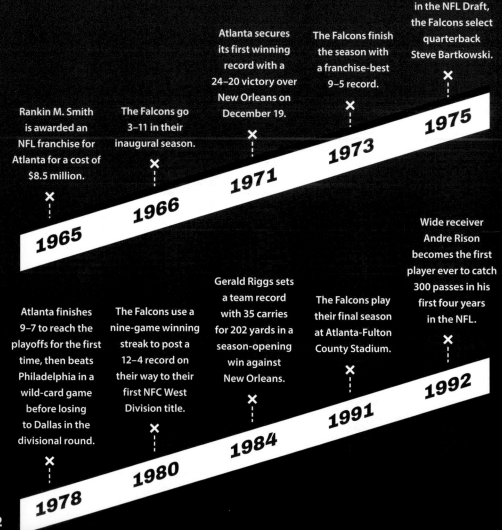

Rankin M. Smith is awarded an NFL franchise for Atlanta for a cost of $8.5 million.

1965

The Falcons go 3–11 in their inaugural season.

1966

Atlanta secures its first winning record with a 24–20 victory over New Orleans on December 19.

1971

The Falcons finish the season with a franchise-best 9–5 record.

1973

With the first pick in the NFL Draft, the Falcons select quarterback Steve Bartkowski.

1975

Atlanta finishes 9–7 to reach the playoffs for the first time, then beats Philadelphia in a wild-card game before losing to Dallas in the divisional round.

1978

The Falcons use a nine-game winning streak to post a 12–4 record on their way to their first NFC West Division title.

1980

Gerald Riggs sets a team record with 35 carries for 202 yards in a season-opening win against New Orleans.

1984

The Falcons play their final season at Atlanta-Fulton County Stadium.

1991

Wide receiver Andre Rison becomes the first player ever to catch 300 passes in his first four years in the NFL.

1992

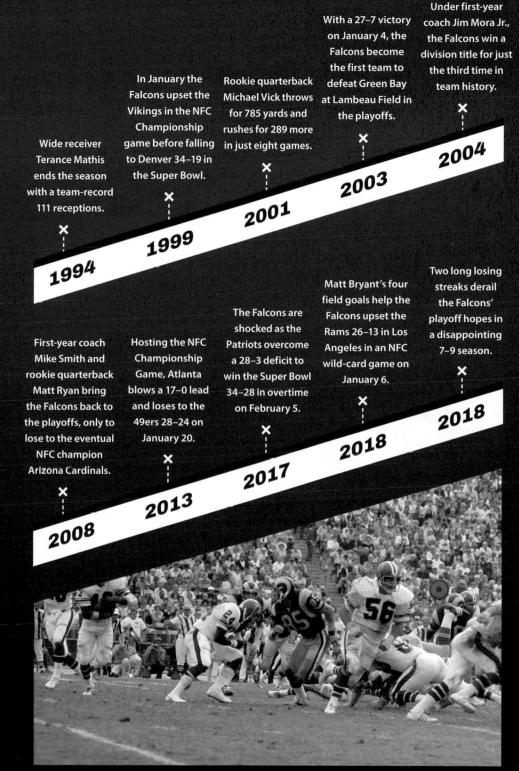

Wide receiver Terance Mathis ends the season with a team-record 111 receptions.

In January the Falcons upset the Vikings in the NFC Championship game before falling to Denver 34–19 in the Super Bowl.

Rookie quarterback Michael Vick throws for 785 yards and rushes for 289 more in just eight games.

With a 27–7 victory on January 4, the Falcons become the first team to defeat Green Bay at Lambeau Field in the playoffs.

Under first-year coach Jim Mora Jr., the Falcons win a division title for just the third time in team history.

1994

1999

2001

2003

2004

First-year coach Mike Smith and rookie quarterback Matt Ryan bring the Falcons back to the playoffs, only to lose to the eventual NFC champion Arizona Cardinals.

Hosting the NFC Championship Game, Atlanta blows a 17–0 lead and loses to the 49ers 28–24 on January 20.

The Falcons are shocked as the Patriots overcome a 28–3 deficit to win the Super Bowl 34–28 in overtime on February 5.

Matt Bryant's four field goals help the Falcons upset the Rams 26–13 in Los Angeles in an NFC wild-card game on January 6.

Two long losing streaks derail the Falcons' playoff hopes in a disappointing 7–9 season.

2008

2013

2017

2018

2018

QUICK STATS

FRANCHISE HISTORY

1966–

SUPER BOWLS

1998 (XXXIII), 2016 (LI)

NFC CHAMPIONSHIP GAMES *(since 1970 AFL-NFL merger)*

1998, 2004, 2012, 2016

DIVISION CHAMPIONSHIPS *(since 1970 AFL-NFL merger)*

1980, 1998, 2004, 2010, 2012, 2016

KEY COACHES

Leeman Bennett (1977–82): 46–41, 1–3 (playoffs)
Dan Reeves (1997–2003): 49–59–1, 3–2 (playoffs)
Mike Smith (2008–14): 66–46, 1–4 (playoffs)

KEY PLAYERS *(position, seasons with team)*

William Andrews (FB, 1979–83, 1986)
Steve Bartkowski (QB, 1975–85)
Bill Fralic (G, 1985–92)
Claude Humphrey (DE, 1968–74, 1976–78)
Julio Jones (WR, 2011–)
Mike Kenn (T, 1978–94)
Terance Mathis (WR, 1994–2001)
Tommy Nobis (LB, 1966–76)
Matt Ryan (QB, 2008–)
Gerald Riggs (RB, 1982–88)
Andre Rison (WR, 1990–94)
Deion Sanders (CB/KR/PR, 1989–93)
Jessie Tuggle (LB, 1987–2000)
Jeff Van Note (C, 1969–86)
Michael Vick (QB, 2001–06)

HOME FIELDS

Mercedes-Benz Stadium (2017–)
Georgia Dome (1992–2016)
Atlanta-Fulton County Stadium (1966–91)

*All statistics through 2018 season

QUOTES AND
ANECDOTES

"I'm gonna ask for so much money, the Falcons are gonna have to put me on layaway."

—Deion Sanders, after being selected fifth overall in the 1989 NFL Draft. Previously, the flashy Sanders had arrived at his final college game at Florida State University in a limousine, wearing a top hat and coattails.

In 1977 Atlanta's defense took on a flavor rich in the southern tradition. Coach Leeman Bennett's defense was given the nickname of "Grits Blitz" on its way to allowing fewer than 10 points per game. The "Grits Blitz" allowed defensive players to rush the quarterback from nearly any position. The Falcons allowed just 129 points in 14 games that season. Grits are a southern breakfast staple, similar to porridge and made of ground corn.

"I am best described as a 'people coach.' I believe in knowing our people and going from there. People play the game, not Xs and Os."

—Leeman Bennett, who took over as head coach in 1977 and led the Falcons to their first NFC West Division title in 1978

"Your choice: It's a victim's mentality or a warrior mentality. It's like, 'I know this run is going to be long, and it's going to be really hard. But here I go again.'"

—Falcons head coach Dan Quinn on the attitude his team needs to have to get over the Super Bowl LI collapse

GLOSSARY

contender
A person or team that has a good chance at winning a championship.

contract
An agreement to play for a certain team.

coordinator
An assistant coach who is in charge of the offense or defense.

defensive backs
The defensive players—cornerbacks and safeties—who start the play farthest from the line.

draft
A system that allows teams to acquire new players coming into a league.

franchise
A sports organization, including the top-level team and all minor league affiliates.

goal line
The edge of the end zone that a player must cross with the ball to score a touchdown.

Pro Bowl
The NFL's all-star game, in which the best players in the league compete.

rookie
A professional athlete in his or her first year of competition.

two-point conversion
An option for teams that have scored a touchdown to try a running or passing play from the 2-yard line for two points, instead of kicking for one point.

MORE INFORMATION

BOOKS

Dupuis-Perez, Lauren, and Katie Gillespie. *Atlanta Falcons*. New York: AV2 by
Weigl, 2018.

Ervin, Phil. *Atlanta Falcons*. Minneapolis, MN: Abdo Publishing, 2017.

Lajiness, Katie. *Atlanta Falcons*. Minneapolis, MN: Abdo Publishing, 2017.

ONLINE RESOURCES

To learn more about the Atlanta Falcons, visit
abdobooklinks.com or scan this QR code. These links are
routinely monitored and updated to provide the most current
information available.

PLACE TO VISIT

Mercedes-Benz Stadium
1 AMB Drive NW
Atlanta, GA 30313
470–341–5000
mercedesbenzstadium.com

Mercedes-Benz Stadium opened in 2017 and hosts all Falcons home games.
The stadium offers tours and has a team store. Atlanta United FC of Major
League Soccer also plays its home games at the stadium.

INDEX

Alford, Robert, 8
Andersen, Morten, 33
Anderson, Jamal, 31, 32
Andrews, William, 22–23, 24

Bartkowski, Steve, 18, 20, 21, 22–23
Bennett, Leeman, 17, 18–20
Blank, Arthur, 34
Bryant, Matt, 39

Campbell, Marion, 17
Chandler, Chris, 30, 32
Coleman, Tevin, 9

Douglas, Harry, 39

Francis, Wallace, 22
Freeman, Devonta, 8

Glanville, Jerry, 20, 26, 29
Gonzalez, Tony, 39

Hampton, Dave, 17
Hebert, Bobby, 30
Hecker, Norb, 14–16
Hooper, Austin, 8
Humphrey, Claude, 18

Jackson, Alfred, 22
Jackson, Steven, 40
Jenkins, Alfred, 22
Jones, Deion, 8
Jones, Julio, 6–7, 41
Jones, June, 29–30

Lawrence, Rolland, 18

Mathis, Terance, 30
Miller, Chris, 28
Mora, Jim Jr., 36

Nobis, Tommy, 14

Quinn, Dan, 6, 41

Reeves, Dan, 30, 36
Riggs, Gerald, 24, 28
Rison, Andre, 28–29
Ryan, Matt, 4–6, 8, 9, 11, 37–39, 41

Sanders, Deion, 28
Santiago, O. J., 30–31
Sanu, Mohamed, 7
Smith, Mike, 6, 37, 41
Smith, Rankin M., 12–14, 16, 34

Turner, Michael, 37, 40

Umenyiora, Osi, 40

Van Brocklin, Norm, 16–17

Vick, Michael, 34–37

White, Roddy, 37

ABOUT THE AUTHOR

Robert Cooper is a retired law enforcement officer and lifelong NFL fan. He and his wife live in Seattle near their only son and two grandchildren.